Present Like A Pro
for Networkers

WHEN YOUR PRESENTATION FEELS LIKE A CONVERSATION, YOU HAVE ARRIVED.

-Lerrod E. Smalls

Present Like A Pro for Networkers

ELIMINATE FEAR, CLOSE THE ROOM, AND RISE TO THE TOP IN NETWORK MARKETING

LERROD E. SMALLS

Brooklyn, NY

About Present Like A Pro

http://PresentLikeAPro.net was developed to be a FREE resource to help all distributors of Multi-Level Marketing, acquire the necessary skill of delivering effective presentations. We are excited about sharing training videos and strategy guides to help you rise through the ranks in our industry.

For information on printing a custom edition of Present Like A Pro for Networkers, please email SpeakUp@PresentLikeAPro.net

QUANTITY DISCOUNT PROGRAM

Our goal is to get this book into the hands of as many people as possible. We have created a quantity discount program that offers leaders that are interested in building huge teams of powerful independent distributors, confidently speaking up in front of rooms all around the world. We suggest that you get copies for new partners, your entire organization, and have them available at all of your events.

1-9 --- $12 each
10-24 --- $10 each
25-49 --- $8 each
50-99 --- $7 each
100-499 --- $6 each
500-999 --- $5 each
1000+ --- $4 each

Bulk book orders are available at http://PresentLikeAPro.net/Store

Feel free to submit questions or requests for engagements to SpeakUp@PresentLikeAPro.net

Dedication

This book is dedicated to my children—God's greatest blessings; my 1st son Lerrod E. Smalls II, my princess London Arielle Smalls, and my youngest Lathan Quaid Smalls. I pray that you will learn from every strategy, failure, success, and experience I have harvested. Use them as steppingstones, placing you higher and happier than was ever possible for me.

May God richly bless you.

Lerrod Smalls is an engaging, action-oriented speaker with a powerful message for entrepreneurs. I have watched Lerrod's growth as a leader in this industry and I must say it is impressive. He has written a very inspiring book with relevant success strategies about how to deliver effective presentations for any MLM business.

This is more than a motivational book—it is a realistic and life changing resource tool that anyone can utilize as a guide to reach the highest levels of direct marketing.

-Barry L Donalson, CDSP
Author, Speaker, and Global Entrepreneur

Acknowledgements

> *"We rise tall in this world not because of the heights of our accomplishments, but because of the shoulders of giants that we stand on... So watch your heels."*

-Lerrod Smalls

First, I must give all due praise to the most high. Thank you GOD, for without your unmerited favor, my unworthiness would have blocked all of the blessings I have enjoyed in my life.

Highest honors to my mother, Juanelle. Although your body has not been seen since 1996, the residual effects of your selfless devotion as a parent, mentor, and friend can be seen in all the good that I am and ever will become.

To my loving wife, Qahira, who took a gamble on a dreamer. You are exactly who you promised you would be the day we got married; that in itself deserves my undying dedication. This world is big and beautiful, and I am looking forward to experiencing all of it with you.

Thanks to my dad, Rodney Smalls, for proving that a life of freedom is possible for me. You have broken the barrier between having an ordinary life and being extraordinary in our family.

To my late grandparents and my many aunts, uncles, cousins, sisters, and brothers bound through blood and through love, I am blessed to call you family. It's my experiences with you that have shaped my thinking of who I could be. I hope you will be proud of your work.

Very special acknowledgement to my mother-in-law Gloria, who has sacrificed so much over the years to help make me shine. For whatever reason, you have chosen to be my biggest fan, and I am truly grateful. To my aunt Lynelle Mahon, who continued the work as my mother when no one else could or would have taken on the job. As long as I should have, so shall you.

Huge thanks to Roberto Knight and Kevin Johnson, two great friends who are always there with the glue to help me fix my train each time I run it off track and crash it into a wall. To my business partners and friends Aquan Donaldson and Geno Moore for always being down for whatever I'm into next. Much thanks to my accountability partners, Chris Kazi Rolle and Kinja Dixon, who always hold me to a higher standard. I must also solute Shanda Holmes and Lesley Hope, who have worn so many hats in helping me become the business of 'Me'.

To my big brother in heaven, Dave "Diamond" Cox, for being the angel on earth that I needed when I was lost in the wilderness. It could have only been you that introduced me to network marketing. You may not read this with your earthly eyes, but I know you are watching from your skybox seat. Your family will always have my support.

My most heartfelt gratitude goes out to all of my students of the Present Like A Pro workshop that have trusted in me all these years, some of which have joined me more than once. I will never take for granted the generosity of your authenticity, having shared so many powerful moments of reflection and storytelling as you become professionals in presenting.

I am, as we all are, a product of our maturation, decisions, and relationships. I am especially grateful for the latter, because without the many helping hands I've received in my life, the magic of my story wouldn't be possible. Thank you.

Foreword

Dr. GEORGE C. FRASER

> "We must come together to create a legacy of economic equality, with new tools to learn, earn, and return."

-Dr. George C. Fraser

Many people never reach massive success when marketing to a network because they fall short of the expertise necessary to do so. My life's work has been connecting people with resources and to one another. I finding opportunities in places others do not simply because I have always been willing to communicate with those I am connected to. My path has led me to teach people all around the world the true value of their network and the best cultivation of relationships. But having lots of friends on social media and a phonebook full of names won't grow your bank account. It has been the process of "Converting Contacts into Contracts" that has me teaching from so many different stages.

We must understand that the sharing of knowledge and presenting of ideas is how our species came to dominate this world, and our further growth as a community can be stunted by our inability to sell one another on new opportunities.

As founder of the *Power*Networking Conference, every year I get to meet many excellent change-makers from all around the world. I was first introduced to Lerrod as an excited participant. Since our 1st conversation, he has utilized my principles to establish and maintain our relationship, keeping me up to date on his developments and various accomplishments. He continually reminds me that it was the formula he learned on human connection in my book *Click* that helped him create explosive growth in his organization. I am proud of the special skills he has mastered in the area of presenting; therefore, I am excited to be a part of this book.

I suggest you pay close attention as he shares with you the tools he has used to win in business. After digesting the strategies presented in this work, I know without a doubt that it will help those on the path to overcome many obstacles in their communication and succeed.

Present Like A Pro for Networkers is a how-to guide which contains everything you need to know about sharing your business, products, and systems with others. Brimming with straightforward strategies, anyone can use it to overcome fears associated with public speaking and presenting their MLM business.

As a guide, this is the one book I'd recommend to those sleeping giants looking for a breakthrough in their presentation power. It's rare to find such practical and concise advice in an easy-to-read format. This book is sure to become a powerful resource for marketers of every company in the direct sales arena. I confidently believe that entrepreneurs wanting to share their vision of a better future, as professionals in this outstanding industry, can benefit from the down-to-earth knowledge presented here.

I say read on.

George

Contents

Foreword...xvii

Introduction: What to Expect of this Book............................1

Chapter One: The 'Why' Behind this Book............................5

Chapter Two: Fear is a Choice..11

Chapter Three: Create Courage with Strategies..................19

Chapter Four: Training the Tongue......................................25

Chapter Five: Are You Selling or Training?.........................31

Chapter Six: Know Your Deal!...35

Chapter Seven: Location, Location, Location......................39

Chapter Eight: Stand and Deliver..45

Chapter Nine: Intro is Everything..53

Chapter Ten: Body Language..61

Chapter Eleven: Issues...69

Chapter Twelve: Get What You Came For............................75

Chapter Thirteen: Wrap Up the Room..................................85

Chapter Fourteen: When You Know Better,
   You Grow Better..97

Chapter Fifteen: Leadership..103

Chapter Sixteen: Last Words...109

Bonus Chapter:...111

About the Author..117

About Dr. George Fraser..121

Credits...127

Contact Information..131

Introduction
What to Expect of this Book

> *"First things first, second things never. Because you should never be doing a second thing first. When the time comes that you have completed the first thing, now the second thing becomes the first thing that you do."*

-Dr. George C. Fraser

You Are Here

You've already read the title of this book, so it's safe to say that by flipping open the cover and getting to this page, you have an interest in network marketing and becoming a champion presenter. Some old guy in our industry once said: "The man with the marker makes the most money!" Being that women dominate the population of participants in our industry, I'm sure he meant to include them as well. Since the days of flip boards and charts on stands, right up through today's sophisticated multimedia PowerPoint presentations and webinars, it has been proven that he or she who presents the information most often and most effectively cashes the big checks.

The benefits of being a great speaker don't stop at recognition, money, or position level. Although these are all great things, having a "million dollar mouthpiece" with even subpar charisma can open doors to places and opportunities you would never have even dreamed were possible. As a public speaker, there are plenty of opportunities waiting for you in corporate America, civil service, and community work, but here we'll discuss specifically how this skill will make you a winner in network marketing.

However, any career that offers you control of your time, unlimited income potential, and the right to work from home is going to require something of you. At some point, you will need to show your plan publicly to various sized groups or do private trainings for your team, duplicating the process of building this business. For these reasons, you need to be very effective at delivering a presentation if you ever hope to be one of the 'rock star' income earners of your company.

> *"Both desire and imagination are stored in the mind of the individual and when stretched, both have the potential to position a person for greatness."*
>
> -Eric Thomas

Mastering these skills will be life changing. Here are just some of the other powerful steppingstones you will look down from as you polish your presentation skills.

- Doing presentations boosts your self-esteem, helping you to share with confidence.

- You earn the trust of others that connect with the value of your business. With this, people will buy from you, trust you, and join you as a distributor!

- In time, you will become a more organized thinker with a smooth delivery.

- Every time you speak up in front of people, you further recognize your own potential and begin to explore more of the greatness in yourself.

- Challenging as it is, speaking at home parties, private receptions, hotel meetings, and even company conventions will unlock other hidden hesitations and fears for you to conquer.

Please understand, this is not some generic "Public Speaking for Idiots" book. We will be discussing the opportunities and challenges faced by networkers, more clearly defined as people in the multi-level marketing or direct sales industry. Throughout this book, I will interchange the term 'audience' with 'guests' or 'prospects' quite loosely, as in our industry, these terms refer to those we wish to share our products and opportunities with.

When you have the command of a room, you have the ability to mold the beliefs and perceptions of others. With talented speaking, you can guide them to do things they never imagined they could, all based on the advice you've given them. This is real influence, and it can be extremely dangerous behind the voice of an Adolf Hitler, or an inspirational power behind the voice of a Dr. Martin Luther King Jr.

Although your goal in presenting may not have such a dramatic effect on the planet as the aforementioned, you still have a responsibility to be genuine, authentic, and clear with your audience. Be clear about what your intentions are and how your offer should be taken seriously. I'm known for bringing lots of humor to the conversation, but I can never forget that presenting is serious work; you should always remember this.

OK, no more chitchat. If you're ready, then let's do this... together.

Chapter One
The 'Why' Behind this B o o k

My kids picked up a saying in school: sharing is caring. I liked it so much that I'm going to start this book off on that note. After years of experience in training individuals through my Present Like A Pro workshop, a few very important questions always seem to be asked by my students:

- Are great speakers born or developed?
- Must all leaders be good speakers?
- Can I build a profitable network marketing business without speaking to a large audience?

So, because I'm caring, I'm going to be sharing my story.

In college, I courageously signed up for public speaking as an elective, and failed it in a most spectacular fashion. It was clear that public speaking was not for me, and I further proved this to myself by refusing to speak at my own mother's funeral. Sheesh.

I finished school in the recommended 4 years, then obtained and lost a high- paying corporate job on Wall Street after only 5 years.

I'm still struggling with the math in that equation. I was blessed to have built two successful businesses with upwards of 20 employees, and from time to time was called upon to say a few words when accepting the occasional success commendation at events, on radio, and even for a TV interview. It was not until I joined network marketing that I was challenged to face my fears and stand in front of people to deliver a presentation.

A friend that I respected very much introduced me to network marketing. I was very reluctant to go see this 'thing' he tried over and over again to get me to see. I was the classic 'know- it- all entrepreneur' prospect that didn't want to waste my time.

This went on until the correct mix of timing and trickery placed me at the DoubleTree hotel in Times Square in NYC. We arrived late; we sat on the last row in the back of the room and could barely decipher what the company was offering. But the presenter was exciting! He had a super confident grin on his face and real passion in his voice about this millionaire factory of a company. The energy in the room was electrified by this gentlemen's presentation style. Long story made short, I got in.

What's relevant to the subject of this book is that I followed the company's plan to the letter. I asked everyone I knew if they were interested in making or saving money with our business. If they said yes, I would invite them to a meeting where my upline leader would come and present the deal. Most times he was available, and the few times he wasn't, I was fairly successful.

Using this method, I received all of the company's Fast Start Bonuses. Then one Sunday afternoon meeting— which as I recall was going according to plan—changed everything. I had everyone in the living room of my new partner's house, lined up on the sofa and ready for action. I set up the presentation DVD and everyone was watching a video showcasing the lifestyle of our big money makers. I introduced my upline leader as the speaker when he said to me, "You're going to do the first part," and then he just walked out!

Even today, as I write this, I can recall the sound of the door closing like the slam of a jail cell gate in one of those "Scared Straight" videos. I would have chased him down and held up the whole meeting if not for one of the guest blurting out, "Hey Smalls, you go ahead and tell us about this thing."

Immediately my hands got sweaty and my throat dried up. My voice was cracking as I spent the first few minutes complaining about how I was going to "get that guy". Then I realized... they were laughing. And they weren't laughing *at* me, they were laughing *with* me.

That was enough to encourage me to click to the first slide of the presentation. I did my best from what I remembered hearing in other presentations by just reading off the screen. And before I knew it, I was at the point where my upline, who was silently listening from the hallway, came bursting in clapping. He wrapped up the details that I missed and closed the meeting out. The end result was two of our five guests signing an enrollment application complete with credit card info – BOOM!

What happened next is not uncommon in this business. I realized that *I could do this*. Although the next few months of presentations were not my most stellar performances, I kept improving. Soon, I no longer needed my champion upline leader to do the presentation. The more planned and impromptu presentations I did, the more new partners signed up. And now, without notice or planning, hesitation or doubt, I confidently share my gift with audiences large and small on a variety of subjects inside and outside of my career as a networker.

As network marketers, our real opportunity is to share the business with as many people as we possibly can. Your company and our industry are not for everyone, so we must always be showing the plan and training the existing team. Therefore, to leverage the use of time and achieve our goals quickly, we must master the art of sharing with large groups of people at one time. That's the big idea behind this book.

↘NOTES

Chapter Two
Fear is a Choice

t's a fact, most people are afraid of public speaking on some level. Those real, honest folks will admit to being terrified. Everyone believes Seinfeld, right?

> *"According to most studies, people's number one fear is public speaking. Number two is death. Death is number two. Does that sound right? This means to the average person, if you go to a funeral, you're better off in the casket than doing the eulogy."*

-Jerry Seinfeld

There is a technical term for this problem; it's called glossophobia. Wikipedia defines this as speech anxiety, being the fear of public speaking or of speaking in general.

Symptoms include:

11

•Intense anxiety prior to, or simply at the thought of, having to verbally communicate with any group.

•Avoidance of events which focus the group's attention on individuals in attendance.

•Physical distress, nausea, or feelings of panic in such circumstances.

Stage fright may also be a symptom of glossophobia (Wikipedia, 2015).

Here come all the big fancy words. Symptoms are the manifestation from the impact of a disease or sickness. Thus, if you or your business partners are human, there is a good chance that either you or they (or maybe both) possibly suffer from this mental affliction. *But guess what?* It's 100% curable! As a matter of fact, some people go from being terrified of a small audience to becoming masters of the microphone, sharing their stories and building incredible organizations worldwide.

The very first step I take with any client or group when discussing their fear of public speaking is to begin understanding what's really going on with them. Then, for all the money they pay me, I tell them the most important thing they will ever need to know, but it is such a cliché that most can't get it at first. "It's all in your head!"

That's it! Think about it. You are afraid *before* you speak, *before* you see the audience, *before* you ever know what the end result will be. Your deep concern is about something in the future that *has not* happened yet, may *never* happen, and most likely *will never* ever happen.

The best acronym I've heard for the word F.E.A.R. is this:

FALSE – EVIDENCE – APPEARING – REAL

If you were ever afraid of public speaking before this book, I am about to give you a huge gift that could be worth millions of dollars and a new life to you. I discovered it in a film, with a story written by Oscar-nominated actor Will Smith, called *After Earth*. Will Smith and his son co-star in this thrilling Sci-Fi adventure movie as soldiers called rangers. The relevant part happens when Will Smith's character tells a story to his son about the time he was attacked by a blind but fear-sensing alien. During a near death experience from the conflict, he was distracted by something beautiful, and in that moment the monster could no longer detect him. He realized the most valuable lesson of his life, and shares it:

> *"Every single decision we make will be life or death. But if we are going to survive this, you must realize that fear is not real. It is a product of thoughts you create. Do not misunderstand me, danger is very real, but fear is a choice."*

-Will Smith

This is your new mantra! Lock it in your mind. "Danger is real, <u>but fear is a choice</u>." You should say it every time you're about to share with a group. You can also visit PresentLikePro.net (shameless plug) and pick up a reminder bracelet. Acquire whatever physical reminder works best for you to be in the right state of mind. Then repeat the phrase, over and over, until you believe it in your heart. And when you're fully engaged, tell yourself without a shadow of doubt, *"I DON'T CHOOSE FEAR!"*

Now ask yourself this question: Are the feelings you're having in your stomach and body a response to any actual *real* threat of danger? No, they are not. Before you deliver a presentation or even think about your upcoming home/business party, ask yourself, *"Is anyone here going to do something dangerous?"* Will there be a gun, knife, or bomb present? **No!** So if there is no *real* eminent physical threat or danger, what is there to be afraid of? The answer is nothing. Again, it is all in your head.

A piece of advice for you intellectuals who stall on your grand opening event or have never made it to the front of the room because you're still trying to *rationalize* how to do what I'm saying instead of actually *doing* it: this is an experience-based business. In other words, "earn while you learn." You will never know it all or be perfect at it. Getting out there and simply doing it grows you, which grows your bank account.

Rhetorical question: Are you ready to grow a massive organization of insanely confidant partners who are relentlessly performing regular exposures and causing your team to grow exponentially? Yes or Yes? Great! Then duplicate these few strategies in a training with your new (and quite possibly shy) distributors. DONE.

↘NOTES

Chapter Three
Create Courage with Strategies

Proven Things You Can Do to Build Confidence

For my shy newbies, be aware that the idea of speaking to family and friends about a business opportunity or products may appear painful, but this will go away as you increase your confidence in sharing. Self-confidence really matters, and those that have it have the advantage. If you think you do not have it, then it's never too late to get it. Here are some things you could do to gradually grow the courage necessary to speak in front of an audience with ease.

- **Speak with more people**

    You will get better not only by talking with a huge crowd, but through simple acts such as going out, leading a conversation, or talking to new people. Simple as it may seem, leading a conversation with people you barely know improves your speaking skills.

- **Pump yourself up**

Being positive is the start to a great opportunity when meeting or training. As you face the audience, drown the butterflies in your stomach with water. Remember that you are the one they came to see and you are a champion. Don't attempt this from a place of trying to be cool. You have to really become your own raving grandparent fan at the little league game of yourself for this to work.

- **Dress for success**

See to it that you dress appropriately and comfortably. When you feel good about how you look, you will be ready to face people and share your story. Be mindful that you should not create a distraction from your message with your outfit. Ladies must be sophisticated yet simple. Gentlemen should be distinguished with a look that isn't overpowering to your guests.

- **Be punctual**

Arrive as early as possible to the venue, earlier than the audience. When you arrive, look around and feel the audience as if they are present. This practice will help you relax. One of my favorite speakers, Les Brown, always shares that he arrives early to events so he can shake hands with the guests. He claims that it makes him less nervous and causes them think twice about boo-ing a guy they just met. Now isn't that hilarious?!

- **The reset**

There may be moments when you feel your throat dry up; just take a sip of water. When you're running out of breath due to nervousness, breathe deeply. When you begin to stutter, pause and gather your thoughts. Whenever things are unfavorable, simply take a step back, give a huge smile, and start again without an apology.

- **When you move, they move**

To express your emotions, appeal to your audience through gestures and eye contact, but be deliberate. Only and always make moves and gestures intentionally so that when you apply them, people get your point. People tend to be involuntary, reactionary creatures. If you nod at someone in the seats, they will nod back. Raising your hand to get confirmation and group participation will cause them to do the same. Bottom line—if you want them to agree, you agree first. They will follow the leader.

Additionally, be sure to maintain a comfortable distance from your front row guests; stay out of their personal space. And perhaps most importantly, never put your back to the group. There is some fancy psychological reason why you shouldn't do this, but let's keep it simple and just say that people don't like it.

- **Practice**

Grab every chance you get to speak in the front of the room! It's your stage; you can make a difference. Schedule a meeting now!

Let's change the world with words.

⬂NOTES

Chapter Four
Training the Tongue

There are some naturally born talented speakers out there; I certainly can't deny that they exist. But to succeed in this industry and grow your business, <u>must</u> you be born like them, with the gift of a golden tongue? Again, the answer is " No". Well, of course there are advantages to having it come naturally, but you shouldn't dwell on that lest you give up your opportunity to grow into a great presenter.

There are trainings that can help you improve your public speaking potential. When you' re eager to learn and determined to push yourself to the room with a view, when it comes to speaking in front of an audience, why not get yourself professionally trained? I have enjoyed and learned from being a part of local Toastmasters events, attending speaker conferences, selling from stage seminars, and mentorship from afar through CD/DVD programs. Don't discount the knowledge that can be gained by purchasing the packaged wisdom of those before you. Here are some steps you can take to become better trained.

- **Meet a coach and seek help**

There are people who have earned a formal education in public speaking and writing. Seek help from someone you think would be a person of credibility and experience. With a good coach on your team, you're sure to learn plenty of new techniques and tips of the trade, which are always beneficial.

- **Stay optimistic**

It pays to identify your mistakes or flaws, but when training to speak in front of a room, you have to condition yourself to a certain level of optimism. This means that you are striving to improve, but you need not worry about the errors you make. Treat this as a free room for learning when you are still in the training phase. Don't be too harsh on yourself, and be open with what is on deck for you. When you're too strict with yourself, you create a pressure that is not going to be helpful. You have to remind yourself that you are doing better each day and 'rock star status' is on its way.

> *"Rome wasn't built in a day, but they were laying bricks every hour."*

-James Heyward

- **Be you, please**

In your Jedi-like training for mastery in our focus of public speaking, do not try and mold yourself into the Yoda you have found. You *must* be yourself. You could be the best within your own means and potentials. Remind yourself that you are going to be a better you. By the way, because you are taking the time to read this book and study how to **Present Like A Pro**, I think you're pretty awesome!

↘NOTES

Chapter Five
Are You Selling or Training?

Top professionals in network marketing are regularly called upon to deliver two types of presentations: persuasive and informative. They both have very different objectives and require polar opposite techniques to deliver.

Persuasive:

- A presentation with the intention of creating a purchase or

  the adoption of an idea.

  Example: Conversations focused around selling your product or sharing an opportunity so that others may join.

Informative:

- A presentation with the goal of informing, teaching, or helping to develop skills in a particular area.

  Example: Training given to your organization or team on the process of recruiting partners or selling your product.

I have given over a thousand presentations in my career, and my experience has taught me that the most powerful MLM opportunity presentations are a careful balance of both types. We must confidently inform and teach our audience about the facts of our industry, company, products, and services. Meanwhile, we should also delicately influence their opinion with our values, personal testimonies, and fears of loss.

Over the years, I have observed so many presentations by champion speakers representing different companies, all with unique offerings. What I can say about all of the most compelling meetings is that they appear as a back and forth dance, a delivery between firm statements of truth and soft sentiments of belief. Simply said, you must speak and adjust your posture to powerfully and confidently present your company's history, products, services, and anything else that's not debatable. At the same time, you should comfortably and persuasively shower your prospects with comments about why you have the golden ticket and what's in it for them.

So the answer to the question that starts off this chapter is:

BOTH.

⬊NOTES

Chapter Six
Know Your Deal!

"You better think before you open your mouth, son."

-Momma

f you were tasked with doing an upcoming brain surgery, taking for granted that you are NOT one of the few brain surgeons in the world, would you spend a significant amount of time beforehand learning about the brain? Yes, of course you would! Without all the blood and pressure from this life- or-death scenario, the same rules apply when you're doing a presentation. Consider the magnitude of what you're doing as you deliver a sales presentation on the most amazing company in the world! You do believe that <u>your company</u> is the best, right? Absolutely, you say? Great! Then the first thing you must do is study the corporately-developed presentation.

Start by doing research on the top performers and high achievers. Locate any videos online or visit live presentations where they will be performing their pitch.

Be ready to take notes and be mindful to watch for all the minor details of things we talk about in this book. Researching in this way will let you gather strategies and phrases you can use to make your unique presentation good just before it's great. Even though you will be learning from them, please remember that you are not a parrot, and so your goal is not to impersonate these leaders.

Next, get the materials required to do a presentation. Most companies use slide shows, videos, poster boards, or at least handouts. Visuals make it much easier for a speaker to express ideas and maintain continuity throughout the presentation. It's your job to know each piece and the order in which it is shown. Even more important, you must know the story that each visual was intended to express. By mastering the latter, there will be no need for mindless memorization, which is boring anyway. Your exposure will always be better fresh and hot, like NYC brick oven pizza!

These ideas reign true for any type of public speaking. Before you rise up to speak with any audience on any topic, especially your MLM opportunity, you need to be well-studied in the presentation. Everyone is counting on you! This includes your partners, your upline leaders, and most importantly your guests. So you need to know your stuff!

↘NOTES

Chapter Seven
Location, Location, Location

Choosing the Best Place for Your Presentation

M any factors add up to a successful presentation, and one of the most overlooked is choosing the right setting. Would you present just anywhere? How can choosing the right location help you? It only makes sense to pick a place that gives you the advantage, a venue that enhances your credibility and leaves a good lasting impression on your audience. Let's spend some time discussing how you can select the right location.

- **Choose a venue that you know**

This simple strategy is an effective timesaver. For one, you can approximate the amount of time you'll need to get there. For another, you'll know where everything is—the restrooms, the power sockets, the projector screen, the air conditioning controls, and so on. You won't have to interrupt your own presentation to look for these things when you need them.

Just be sure to choose a place that your prospective guests also know or can find easily. It would be pretty counter-productive if your participants are late because they had a hard time finding your meeting space. So where is the best place to have an MLM exposure, you ask? The answer is simple: your home, of course! Your guests will feel privileged to be invited, and you most likely won't be late. By the way, when you're on your home turf, you're in control. That boosts your effectiveness tenfold.

If you must present in an unfamiliar place, be sure to arrive extra early to check that everything is in order. It is also wise to have a backup venue nearby in case problems arise, such as your original location becoming unavailable.

- **Choose a place without distractions**

You'll want your prospects to focus on what you're saying when you're saying it—and nothing else. Choose a quiet, relaxing spot away from crowds and loud music. That rules out nightclubs, sporting events, movie theaters, and yes, birthday parties.

Also, be sure to avoid places that have potential distractions. Your prospect's home or office may spell trouble for your presentation when coworkers, children, or even pets interrupt just as you're hitting your stride.

Imagine being in the middle of your spiel when your prospect's secretary barges in with a call for an urgent meeting. Where does that leave your pitch? In the pail!

- **Choose a location that speaks well of your business**

Pick a bright, airy place that gives you a happy and contented feeling. These places relax your client and make them more agreeable. Also, pick a location that distinguishes you as a wealthy, successful person. A country club, a classy restaurant, a fancy hotel lobby, or a posh meeting room with a great view are all excellent places that send a signal that you are someone to be taken seriously. Avoid gloomy, poorly-lit venues filled with cigarette smoke or surly folk. You don't want to give the impression that you're proposing something illegal or dangerous.

Given all the above tips, one of the best places to present may actually be your marketing company's very own headquarters. This gives you a home-court advantage like you wouldn't believe—not only can you use the venue for free, you can also use whatever presentation materials are available. Plus, it shows that your company is a functioning and legitimate business. If your prospect is unable to come to your headquarters or if it is a satellite office, choose a neutral meeting place nearby where you can reference the location.

If distractions aren't enough to deter you, keep in mind that when giving a presentation at your prospect's home or office, you're giving them the advantage that you should have given yourself.

Finally, ask for support from your partners or other company leaders for a space. You'll be surprised what becomes available when you start asking. Your choice of venue affects the outcome of your presentation, so choose well my friend!

⬊NOTES

Chapter Eight
Stand and Deliver

The Keys to the Kingdom of Delivery

"I can show you better than I can tell you."

-Cousin Kenny

After writing and rewriting this chapter several times, I realized that using words on a page to express the feeling of an amazing presentation is the same as trying to describe a gorgeous sunrise to someone who has never seen one. I would love to come out and personally do a live example with all of you. There is no question that one-on-one coaching by a professional can help you step into your greatness as a speaker. But that's not possible at this point. Still, there are some things I want you to become aware of in order to help develop your own powerful speaking style. Start with these tips and grow from there.

- **Be On Time**

  |*"There is nothing else I have to say about that."*

  -Forrest Gump

- **Stay on Time**

Staying aware of your available time is critical, especially in an opportunity meeting where more often than not there's no clear time limit for the presenter. Misjudging this can be a disaster with catastrophic effects such as dozing, texting, leaving, and even snoring! In some cases I have seen a room of guests go from super excited and engaged to slow blinking and dazed in a matter of 15 minutes.

Studies show that people only retain approximately 20% of the information contained in a 60-minute lecture or training, and even less for a sales meeting. During a 90-minute event, most people can muster a pitiful 20 minutes of continuous undivided attention. Most important of all, Dr. Terri D. Fisher contributed her findings on www.psychologytoday.com, claiming that on average the human brain thinks about food, sex, or sleep every 30 minutes. What does this mean for you as a presenter? Time is not your friend, my friend.

Based on my network marketing experience, I can confidently state that you must be clear, concise, engaging, informative, and personable all in under 40 minutes if you want to enjoy the highest closing ratios.

However, there are some presenters that go on for 90 minutes or more in a sales meeting and still have massive success. Just know that it's not common or advised.

The best tip for minding your minutes is to dedicate a timekeeper for your presentation that can flag you as you approach the time you have allotted for the talk. NEVER look at your watch publicly if you want your prospects to keep their attention on you and not the TV show they might be missing for your meeting.

- **Speak up**

Always test the volume of the sound system you will be using or your vocal range if you are in a space without amplified sound. Arrive early and have someone go to the farthest seat in the venue and confirm that they can hear you clearly and smoothly in your normal speaking voice. Although sound is not the biggest factor of a presentation, if your audience can't decipher your words clearly, they'll quickly become annoyed and you will lose their attention fast.

- **'Conversationalize' them**

While I cannot locate this word in the dictionary, it has a very important professional meaning: engage your audience by requiring their participation. People generally dislike lectures, so if your exposure meeting is like a 45- minute broadcast, you may lose some possibly great prospects. There is a balance you must strike between providing information and asking rhetorical questions so that your guests feel as if they are a part of a two- way dialogue. This will only work if you mean it. Try to share a thought, ask a question, and give those in the seats a chance to process and acknowledge to you that they agree. Only ask questions that require a **"YES"** or **"NO"** answer, but keep those hands going up and those heads nodding throughout the conversation. By asking open-ended questions, the responses can vary, which may create unexpected, unfavorable, 'uneverything' results (my other unfound word).

- **Your 'Stride & Glide'**

I won't spend much time on this topic, but it is too important to ignore. From the moment you receive your introduction and take the front of the room, your audience is judging you. Yes, people do still judge a book by its cover. So what can these fine people possibly judge you on before you even open your mouth? An outfit that is crisp, in current fashion, and simple in color will give you the look for who's looking, but there is something else they see. It's all in how you approach!

This is <u>very important,</u> and you should take proper rehearsal to create a powerful, confident, and pleasant stride for your presentation. Even top performers often overlook this, so take it as a slight edge for you to make the difference that can make the difference. Remember, your goal is to be a powerhouse presenter, right? Well, this book isn't "Meetings for Rookies" either. This is **_Present Like A Pro for Networkers!_**

↘NOTES

_____

_____

_____

_____

_____

_____

_____

_____

_____

_____

_____

_____

_____

_____

_____

_____

Chapter Nine
Intro is Everything

I n a boxing match, everyone hangs onto their seat to see the 1st punch. The same goes for your audience in a sales meeting. Open the conversation with a bang and you'll instantly get their attention. This truth is an essential step for your talk. As you deliver what you have prepared, you need to have the attention of your audience the whole way through, but it's going to be much easier if you can capture it right from the start.

How do you do that? Well, every coach has lots of tips on this; some are tried and true, while others are not as common but may be exactly what you need. The following is an exact how-to which can help you leave the impression you want in the first moments of your delivery.

- **Bust down the wall**

After being properly introduced to your audience, you climb the stage and plant your flag in the center. Now what? Those people in the seats are thinking hundreds of thoughts, mostly about the value of their time, and

preparing for the final decision if this experience is going to be a waste of it or not. It is in your best interest to be like the NYPD! You have to arrest, lock up, and convict those things which are creating a disturbance in their heads. This can done with my 3-part method:

GIVE + TAKE + GIVE

1. Give Something Away

- Be transparent and vulnerable about something related to you and why you are presenting this information. Feel free to make fun of yourself; you should have no shortage of content here.

2. Take Something Away

- Express exactly what your big offer is from a visionary perspective, and now that they are exposed to it, there should be no reason why they can't have that thing.

3. Give Them the Rules

- Let them know that if they are not fully engaged or open to your ideas and information, their time will surely be wasted and they will miss out on the possibilities that you are promising.

- **Actions speaks louder than words**

Instead of steadily speaking throughout your speech, you could start your speech with a catchy gesture that is in connection with the speech you are about to deliver. We know what the power of gestures is. For example, when you are to talk about human rights issues, you could start with a strong pound on the podium or a hand gesture showing rejection. This would also prepare the audience's mind for what you are going to talk about.

- **Laughter is the pill**

Boredom is the biggest enemy of any public speaker, especially in our industry, where skepticism is a demon sitting on the shoulder of most of our guests. To interject humor would be a big help in keeping your audience with you until you hear the applause bouncing off the walls and feel a distributor application in your hand. Humor is an asset. Whatever style of speech or conversation you possess, cracking jokes or playing with witty thoughts or remarks is a great opener.

- **Quotable quotes**

You can fill any room with the air of mystic wisdom by using quotes from famous and notable people. If you can recall an impactful line from a well-known author, powerful leader, accomplished actor, or beloved athlete, you will be starting your speech with the approval of truth and validity. Quotes signify a speaker's depth of knowledge and preparation. When you quote people of fame or a person who has relevance to your topic, you show that you are a well-researched and resourceful speaker.

- **Tell it like a story**

I ask people all the time, "Do you remember the year US President Abraham Lincoln died?" Most people answer, "In the 1800's or something, right?" But then I ask, "Do you remember how he died?" Everyone automatically tells me about how Lincoln was assassinated one night in a theater. Why am I telling you this? It means that people can remember stories, but the details and the facts aren't always as important to them. Stories are a hit for people of all ages. When you can attach the strings of a story to your presentation, you will be able to have the audience's attention until you reach your very last slide and tie those strings together. So start your talk off by telling stories that are relevant and interesting; they will be with you from the beginning to the end.

"Never tell a story without a point, and never make a point without a story."

-Les Brown

You only have one shot and a short period of time to give a powerful introduction. It's like racing a sports car down a twisty mountain road—you can think of these tips as your guardrails.

⬎NOTES

Chapter Ten
Body Language

Fun fact: Did you know that in a live presentation, what you are perceiving with your ears is only 10% of the information you register as important? The majority of what we communicate can be found in our vocal tone (30%), in our actions and gestures (60%), and lastly in our words (10%). Your prospects' behavior provides clues as to how they're feeling, which in turn tells you how to deal with it. But body language goes both ways. You must be aware of your own behavior too so as to inspire the best possible reaction from your audience. Keep this in mind while delivering the opportunity of a lifetime.

- **Windows to the soul and doorway to a sale**

The eyes have it! The single most important aspect of body language is looking your prospects right in the eyes. This conveys respect, confidence, trustworthiness, and sincerity. Likewise, not doing so conveys fear, disinterest, a lack of confidence, shame, and secretiveness. However, the look that I'm talking about is not a blank stare or a gaze; this is a solid connection! You must create a moment in time to share with the audience as individuals, where you make true "I see you and you see me" contact with as many of them as visibly possible. If I have 30 minutes to do a presentation with 30 guests in the room, I will make sure each guests gets a minute of my eye-connection through a smooth panning motion.

Please note: When presenting internationally, research the culture of the people you will be sharing with, because some cultures may be an exception.

It is important to maintain eye contact while sharing and building a rapport with your audience. Look at them longer and more often than at your presentation material. And it's absolutely essential to look them in the eye when attempting to close. If your prospects don't want to meet your eyes, it's likely that they're intimidated by you or disinterested in what you have to say. Try to put them at ease by offering small talk. Have a quick diversion on common interests and other things that the majority of people enjoy or care about. However, be mindful not to bring politics, religion, or even sports into the conversation. People get real touchy about certain things, and there is no faster way to lose a connection with your participants than to turn them off in a side conversation.

- **Lead with your arms**

Your arms can convey great emotion. Use grand gestures

to generate excitement, and keep your arms still for quiet, intense moments.

Whatever you do, don't cross your arms. This highly-defensive position conveys anger or indifference. It practically screams, "I don't care." If your prospects cross their arms, they are likely adopting a defensive position toward something you said. Try to re-engage them by shifting the focus back on them and what they want. Get them to participate. Instead of focusing on negative or untrusting thoughts, ask them what they like most about what you've discussed.

- **Mind your head**

Keeping your head at a level, steady position is a sign of confidence and sends the signal that people should listen to you. On the other hand, tilting your head to the side is a sign that you are receptive and ready to listen.

- **Bridging the gap**

As much as possible, sit beside your prospect. Having a desk between you only underscores your initial emotional distance. Bridge it by sitting together and talking as equals, but pay attention to how comfortable he or she is with your distance. If you sense them pulling back from, you may be intruding on their personal space and should back off.

- **Find the right angles**

Simply put, we angle ourselves to face people we like or are attracted to, and angle away from or square up to people who repel us. Face your body toward your prospect while talking to them, tilting or leaning forward in an always-ready-to-listen kind of way. Likewise, when a prospect leans toward you, it means they're interested in what you have to say. Take advantage of this and move through the presentation quickly because this door can close at any minute.

- **Handshakes for dummies**

To begin with, be sure your hands are warm and dry! Nobody likes a cold, clammy hand that shows its owner's nervousness. A firm grip on your handshake shows that you're confident, friendly, and trustworthy. Now again, international customers may require a different approach based on their culture, so know your audience.

When your hands are palms-up, they convey friendliness and openness. Palms down convey dominance and maybe even aggressiveness. This usually comes into play when shaking hands for the first time. It's best to offer a level, upright handshake so as to show you're on equal footing.

- **No fidgeting**

Twitchy, restless legs portray nerves and stress; try to keep them under control by planting both feet on the ground.

As with crossing your arms, crossing your legs is a no-no. The 'Figure 4' (arms and legs crossed) portrays you as arrogant, closed minded, or defensive. When your prospect does this, try to engage him or her in a friendly, non-threatening manner.

In the end, *people like to be liked.* If you give every indication that you like the person across from you, you will receive the same thing back—and it's always easier to present to a friendly audience. This is such a critical component to presenting that we go over it in significant depth during the **Present Like A Pro** live workshop.

↘NOTES

Chapter Eleven
Issues...

f you ever become fortunate enough to find yourself having some one-on-one time with a seasoned professional networker of MLM, do yourself a favor and find out about their wildest in-home presentation story. I personally have experienced things like a drunken heckler blurting out his feelings on MLM—"This is a scam!"—and the 'laughing cow' that continually exaggerated an obnoxiously loud laugh. Oh, I have a book's worth of other catastrophes, too, like the naked baby streaking out of nowhere across the room and knocking over the projector! There is no way to prepare you for every scenario designed to sabotage a presenter, but these tips will help.

- **Be guided by your presentation**

No matter how even the most distracting or hostile audience bombards you with challenges, when you go back to the essence and the content of your presentation, you will always be on target. Surviving a few early distractions confidently will show that you know what you're talking about. If you're using company slides or materials, just keep referring back to them to stay on point in your presentation.

- **Be attentive and understand the questions being raised**

If you notice that a person from the crowd is just asking you questions for the sake of asking questions, do not respond with a sarcastic tongue. No matter how challenging the question is, keep your cool and answer accordingly. I have found that being clear in your opening statement that everyone should hold their questions to the very end works best. From time to time, your audience will forget this agreement, and you can give them a gentle reminder.

- **Be the master of your temper**

Treat your audience as your friends. By doing this, they will feel a sincerity that can lead to establishing a chemistry between you and the audience. No matter how hard a part of the crowd pushes you to be irritated, hold that feeling and remember that you are there to talk— not to argue. Our industry has been around for more than half a century, yet many people are ignorant as to how it works. Respect their confusion or misunderstandings by having patience and smiling as you share.

- **Be honest to goodness**

The more honest you are, the more the audience will really listen to you. It' s easier to deliver a sincere speech than to pretend. If you pretend, the audience will know that you're not being fully truthful, which will hurt your message. If you become known for embellishing, going over the top, and making claims just to capture the crowd's attention, it will block you from the magic of a duplicating team. Your leaders won't bring their precious guests to your presentations, and before you know it, you're presenting to an empty sofa.

- **Be careful with your gestures**

Never use gesture that may signal to the audience that you demand dominion over them or that you're around to preach. Keep your hands to yourself, and never flare your arms when responding. Guard your facial expressions from unintentionally saying something that you don't mean. Safe, smiling, and smooth gestures are always wise options in times of stress. Be expressive but not too powerful.

There are a lot of things to consider when speaking in front of a group, big or small. From the preparation of your event space to the delivery of your talk, there are things to always remind yourself of. When it comes to the challenge of talking to a hostile crowd, would you dare continue speaking? You can, you will, and you must. Just know that each time you overcome an adversity at the microphone, you become better for it. That's what will separate you from the amateurs, and you will **Present Like A Pro**.

↘NOTES

Chapter Twelve
Get What You Came For

Ok, this is quite possibly the longest and most driven chapter of the book. If you didn't skip through the previous chapters, then congratulations! You made it. So now let's do what the title of this chapter says and help you *get what you came for.*

You either started out with a goal to give your team an inspiring motivational speech, train from the stage on the newest points of the compensation plan, or deliver a compelling opportunity presentation. Whatever your reason for climbing this mountain and sharing from the front of the room, at some point the show must come to an end and close. Getting what you came for is about using emotion to lock-in the information you just transferred to your audience. Is it for the focused, determined eyes of your organization, hungry and ready to explode, or the prospects in your meeting with completed application sheets? Either way, you've got to close!

No matter if you call it an opportunity briefing, a challenge party, a chat and chew, a private reception, or a hotel meeting, after guests see your offering, they'll be asking themselves three infamous questions:

1. *Did I understand this?*
2. *Do I believe this?*
3. *Can I do this?*

The more often you can produce a "Yes" to all three questions, the faster you will rise as a champion presenter and high-income earner in your company.

The Best Closing Points Ever

I know that it's quite arrogant and presumptuous of me to go blurting out that I know the best presentation closing points in the world (you're probably thinking something like that right now). Well, just hang on and hear me out. I have compiled and used these points, in full or in part depending on the energy in the room when I arrive, at the end of my presentations. If the energy is low, you might need every single word! But if your energy is high, just focus on getting to a few parts that you like and handing out your enrollment package.

<u>WARNING ABOUT THE FOLLOWING:</u>

This is powerful stuff here! Deliver it as points when closing a presentation or as a script for a conference call. Without a doubt, I can say with conviction that for any meeting, large or small, regardless of your audience's religion, race, or age, this just plain WORKS! I've written it using many bolds and other markings to help guide you in the temperament I recommend. But remember:

"It's your thing, do what you want to do."

-Salt n' Pepper

Start something like this:

I would like everyone to know that I'm truly grateful for the time you have dedicated to seeing this presentation. Although I have been blessed with significant success as a leader in this company, the most important thing to me is the opportunity I have been given to help other people succeed.

Outside of rank and position, I consider my true title in this company to be a **HELPER.** But truth is, I can only help those who want to be helped. So help me by raising your hand and answering a few simple questions.

1. **Does anyone agree that many people are:**
    ○ Drowning in debt?
    ○ Dying of no free time?
    ○ Suffering from unfulfilled lives?

2. To solve this, those people must wantto participate in their own rescue, right?

Many of you may have heard the timeless philosophy:

> *"Give someone a fish and you can feed them for a day. Teach them HOW to fish and you can feed them for a lifetime."*

-the Wise Man

That's great stuff, but as a Helper in this company, I can take it a step further...

> *"Show someone how to buy the POND and generations of their family will never go hungry!"*

-the Wiser Man

So here is the new definition of SELF-FISH—it's **FISHING for YOURSELF!**

Is it time for you to invest in your ownpond?

Many people spend most of their lives becoming experts at fishing to feed other people's families. Getting up every day, rain or shine, they give everything they've got to a job for the sake of building someone else's dream.

Tony Gaskins Jr. said:

> *"If you don't build your dream, someone will hire you to build theirs."*

What if the dream you're participating in changes? That's right: layoffs, restructuring, pay cuts. Call it what you want, but that is the day your nightmare begins.

The great writer and poet Maya Angelou said:

> *"Don't make anyone a priority, when all you are to them is an option."*

The fact of the matter is that **you** have to decide that it's **your** turn! Your dream can come true, but you have to realize that NOBODY is ever going to do it for you!

Ask yourself a question:

Are you fighting for your dreams every day?

Les Brown said:

> *"The moment you stop fighting for what you do want, is the moment what you don't want automatically takes over."*

That means:

- Stop fighting for good health, and OBESITY TAKES OVER.
- Stop fighting for happiness, and SADNESS TAKES OVER.
- Stop fighting for your dreams, and DESPAIR TAKES OVER.

Guess what? There is somebody, somewhere, right now, living

YOUR DREAM!

- They are driving YOUR DREAM CAR.
- They are living in YOUR DREAM HOUSE.
- They are doing all of the things YOU **ONLY DREAM ABOUT**. ONE WORD separates the poor from the wealthy: **ACTION**.

Being poor is only a failure to **ACT**!

It is not the money in your account right now.

The word P.O.O.R. has an acronym:

Passing — Over — Opportunity — Repeatedly

P.O.O.R. is a state of mind... *Have you been living poor until today?*

The action people of the world are the ones who create magic in this life. These are people like:

- Bill Gates
- Oprah Winfrey
- Steve Jobs
- Sir Richard Branson

They too have endured hard times just like you. They've been scared to jump out on faith just like you might be. The difference is **THEY DO IT ANYWAY!**

Everyone wants success, but most are not **WILLING** to take action! It's like wanting to eat, but not being willing to **CHEW**!

The biggest financial divide in this world is not between the haves and the have nots. No, it's really the **wills** and the **will nots**.

Now ask yourself, is this making sense? Someone listening to me right now is going to take massive action and get started right away.

But realistically, some of you will not. I know this because the statistics say 97% of people in the world choose to work for the other 3%. That means only 3% of people took action to go after their dreams, using the other 97% to fulfill them.

I've told everyone who I am and what I stand for, and now I'm curious about who you are.

Have you been *watching things happen* for long enough and are ready to actually *make something happen*?

If you're saying to yourself...

- ***I'm not ready!***
  - Guess what, you'll never be ready.

- ***I don't have time to do this!***
  - Everyone has the same amount of time, it's how you use it that counts. Has the way you've been

spending your time been working for you?

- Everyone can make time for what's important.

• ***I don't have the money to get started!***

- If that's the problem, then it's time to ask yourself the hardest questions:

  - How long have I been living like this?

  - When is it going to change?

  - Who is going to do it for me?

Here is what I know: "Nothing is impossible to a made up mind!" The only thing left to answer is...

How bad do you need a positive change in your life?

More importantly, what are you willing to give up to get it?

After delivering this closing in full or in part, stop talking. Your silence will cause them to reflect and answer the questions in their mind, which will compel them to say something. Remember, the next person to speak after such a riveting barrage of ideas and questions concedes to the other!

⬎NOTES

Chapter Thirteen
Wrap Up the Room

So you've completed what you believe to be a stellar performance. Your guests were engaged throughout the conversation. You hit all of the major points in your business overview, and they're holding the enrollment application or sales sheet in their hands. Now what?

The presentation is not over yet. This is your time to really shine! Your partners and guests will begin to mingle with one another and discuss their decision to take action. As the presenter, you have a major responsibility to field questions and give empowering remarks to those who need just a slight bit of encouragement to get over their jitters. This is the key difference from traditional speeches given by public orators—most MLM meetings must be closed with a personal touch from the presenter. You are now a shining star, a beacon of light in the darkness for your prospects, so you must assist in closing the presentation *like a PRO*.

- **Finding the need**

Of the many networking skills you'll want in your arsenal, showing people why they should join your organization is among the most critical. There is no set formula to do this, however, because each person is different and will want different things—wealth, prestige, family life, wellness, time, freedom, and so on.

One approach many people try is *hard selling*, which we can safely say is hated by just about everyone. Hard selling involves pushing the actual product onto your prospect using the sheer energy of your presentation to override any concerns or objections they may have. This is why many people pretend to not be home when the salesman comes a-knockin' on the door.

Nobody likes being sold! A client may buy your product or service to get you out of their hair, but you'll lose a lot of goodwill and probably the chance to sell to them again, too. It's even more disastrous for building a network because your organization won't have a concrete relationship to stand on. You'll have a cascade of fallouts as soon as you turn your back on your new recruits. The good news is that there is another approach that not only stands a better chance of closing a prospect, but also fosters goodwill and a sense of cooperation.

"Just listen to what they need, then you simply present your business as the best answer to your prospects needs."

-Anthony Robbins

This is the opposite of hard selling. You do less talking and more listening. All you need is some patience, a few good questions, and a sympathetic ear. Your goal is to find your prospect's specific need before positioning your business as a solution. Imagine sitting down with a prospect for the first time. Do you go straight into a presentation? Hardly! You'll want to get to know them first. You try and chat for a while to build rapport. This is an excellent time to ask a few probing questions. Probing is a subtle art; it needs to come from a genuine interest without coming across as nosy. The point is to get the other person talking about themselves. This is usually easy to do since we are our own favorite subject. Steer the conversation towards topics that are important to them. Ask them to elaborate, clarify, and share stories about themselves. Doing so will eventually lead them to talking about what's missing from their lives.

Here are some topics that can help lead towards more meaningful conversation:

Family

- How is your spouse doing?
- How are your children?

- How are your parents?

Career

- How is your career going?

- Does your boss treat you well?

- Do you have time for yourself or your family?

- Are you happy with where you are?

Achievements

- So what's next for you?

- Are you aiming to buy a new home/car/business?

- Are you thinking about retirement? How's that going so far?

You can also steer the topic towards health, children's education, or any present or future expenses. Find out where the problems lie. Maybe they're worried about financing their home. Maybe they're dissatisfied with their paycheck or their job status. Maybe they're burdened with supporting their parents or an unemployed sibling. Maybe they're facing an uncertain financial future. Take the time to sincerely listen, to empathize with your prospect. Let *them* talk. Resist the temptation to jump in with advice. It's important that you understand what they want and show that you're genuinely interested in what they have to say. Only after they've finished talking do you thank them for sharing and then lead into your presentation:

> *"I understand you have these concerns and I'd like to see if I can help. I know of a way that can benefit you financially/career- wise/health-wise, and you can do it at your own time and your own pace. Would you like to hear more about it?"*

When they say yes, proceed to the presentation, making sure to point out how it will indeed help with their concerns. Come from the spirit of wanting to help. Show them that an extra means of leveraged income will solve a majority of their problems, and that you can coach them on how to do it. By establishing a specific need, even after the presentation, you have the basis for a business relationship. Your guest won't feel that you are selling them something; they'll feel as if you are helping them make a wise choice. This means it will be easier to close the deal. In fact, you won't have to convince them—they'll convince themselves!

Now you have to start answering the tough questions from tough prospects. Have you ever met a prospect who flat-out refuses to believe you, anything you say, anything that's in the video, etc.? If you were to offer them a donut, they would refuse it for the hole! Don't turn off the lights on these people. They're so negative, they just might develop! Ok, enough of that. In your career, you will definitely meet those who simply contradict everything you say. You want to get them to see your side and agree with your point of view, but that's an argument.

- **Keep pushing and you'll push them away**

Answering objections is a skill you'll want to learn very early in your network marketing career. The trouble is, even the correct answer may not always get you what you want. People can give objections like "network marketing is a pyramid scam", or "only the people on top get to make money", or "MLMs are illegal businesses", or "only people who already have big networks in place can get rich." Simply telling them the opposite thing may not work at all. You may win the argument, but you will most likely lose the customer.

Nobody likes to be wrong, and nobody likes to be proven wrong. When you push, they'll push back. The harder you push someone to change their mind, the harder they'll try to entrench themselves in their opinion. They may say, "I know I'm right because I know someone who lost a lot of money in MLM."

So if they believe they're right and you can't get them to budge, do you just give up? Of course not! You can use the power of appreciation to get them to see you point of view.

- **Sincerely listen to their side**

The first step in appreciation is to find out where your prospect is coming from. To do this, *you need to make fewer statements and ask more questions*. For example, if your participant says "This business sounds like another pyramid scam", ask them, "What do you mean by pyramid scam?" and "Why do you say that my business is one?"

These questions are not meant to be asked defensively. You'll want them to understand that you're curious about what makes them think that way. You want to sincerely understand their side of the story. Saying things like "Help me understand" or "What makes you say that?" are all meant to probe your prospect's emotions. This attitude allows them relax and let their guard down. Sometimes when you ask someone to clarify their statement, they may see on their own that their opinion is unfounded or inaccurate (e.g., "it's shaped exactly like a pyramid, so I thought it was a pyramid scheme"). If you're lucky, they may even decide to correct themselves all on their own. But even if this doesn't happen, you are still one step closer to an agreement.

- **Appreciate their point of view**

The key aspect of this approach requires as much sincerity as when you were listening: *acknowledge their point of view*. This does not mean you have to agree with them! It simply means that you see the merit of their opinion, even if you don't share it. Spoken truthfully, "I understand how you feel" is a very powerful statement. It means that you understand them, that their side made sense. People will feel that you respected their opinion, and this invites them to respect yours. You can go further by stating that if you were in their shoes, you would probably feel the same way. For example:

> "I understand how you feel. You dropped $500 into an MLM and didn't get your money back. Losing your investment in any business is rough. If it happened to me, I'd feel the same way and wouldn't give network marketing a second thought."

Again, let the signal be clear: you sincerely understand their side. Once they see that, it's easier for the two of you to agree on something. But don't give up at this point, just clearly show them how this was not your reality, and in your company, it's possible for them to have the outcome they desire.

- **Get them to appreciate you**

Now you can move on to stating your side. Get them to see the merit of your point of view. One well-used formula is the *feel, felt, found* method.

> "I understand how you **feel**. I once **felt** that I was terrible at sales and wouldn't even be able to answer a single question the customer would throw at me. But I **found** that the company trains its downlines very well and wouldn't even let me do presentations until I was ready. Also, it was less about selling and more about sharing the benefits of the product with other people."

You can restate something like this

> *"I get what you're saying. I was pretty much the same way when I started. I thought that only the people above me would get rich, and I was going to wind up losing my investment. But I realized that they were personally interested in my development and were willing to help me get my organization going. They taught me everything I needed to know to be successful. Now I'm earning an extra $1,000 a week and I've been nothing but grateful."*

Since you didn't undermine what your prospect said, they'll find it easier to appreciate what you say. Mutual appreciation opens the door to agreement, and is one of the most efficient ways to close a guest. Being a presenter goes far past standing on the stage pontificating. Spewing out fancy jargon just wouldn't cut it in this business. We don't get compensated with applause; we get paid by grateful customers, by way of loyal distributors. That's the difference, that's why we call this ***Present Like A Pro for Networkers***.

↘NOTES

Chapter Fourteen
When You Know Better, You Grow Better

> *"The most important investment you can make is in yourself...the best asset is your own self. You can become, to an enormous degree, the person you want to be."*

-Warren Buffet

- **Invest in your personal growth**

You don't have to speak like a presidential candidate to be an effective presenter in network marketing, It's all about your passion and commitment to your personal best. There have been amazing marketers from all corners of the world, some with little to no formal education, that have nonetheless managed to 'kick butt' in this industry. Consider the world- famous Les Brown, who as a child was labeled mentally retarded and held back twice in grade school, only to go on and become a dominant network marketer in one of the biggest companies of our industry's history. Les Brown has since been recognized by many accredited organizations as one of the greatest public speakers in the world. With no formalized training or college degree, he invested in himself over many years through a variety of training programs until he mastered the art of telling a great story to an audience. He proved you don't need fancy, obscure multi-syllable words to make the crowd buy into your ideas!

This list goes on and on with champions of personal development and speaking like Art Williams, a high school football coach turned founder of the company we know today as Primerica Financial services, and a young farmer boy from Idaho that grew up to be the great Jim Rohn (rest in peace). Please understand that the big point I'm trying to make here is that scholastics, large vocabularies, and university degrees (which are all very good things, by the way) don't make you a powerful presenter in MLM. It's more about mastering the craft of sharing your opportunity from your heart.

"I cannot remember the books I've read any more than the meals I have eaten; even so, they have made me."

-Ralph Waldo Emerson

- **Read Voraciously**

Being a presenter does not mean that you have to rely solely on your power of discussion or your skill in speaking words clearly. Your goal is to share the plan and cast a vision that the benefits of your product or program are of high value for your audience. As you speak, you have to have the tongue of credibility. This can be achieved only by researching facts, numbers, quotes, and relevant information.

For modern times, the internet is a great tool for research. However, always verify your sources and check your facts before using them. There is nothing worse than delivering an amazing presentation and tarnishing it with some confidently blurted out false fact or piece of information. Introducing proven facts and statistics in your speech and quoting your sources will give your presentation tremendous credibility and will bolster your confidence when you close.

If your company allows it, you can even use visuals like copies of articles from websites or newspapers. When people notice that you have exerted effort to prepare your presentation, they will see your business as solid and reliable. With this step, you'll not only inform people of the content of your pitch, but you will introduce them to the possibility that they can share this information, too. Never lose sight of the fact that the true magic of our business is that we learn, share, and duplicate.

Face the crowd with a feeling of certainty that you will not fail them, that you are going to talk, and that what you talk about will not be mere hearsay. You are a gladiator in a suit! Or not. If you have been reading great books and investing in your mind, you will see how this dramatically improves your conversation from the stage. Remember that public speaking in a business presentation could be the gateway to gaining public trust, which is another huge value. In order for you to achieve such a valuable thing, you have to earn it. But how can you do that? Simple! Never stop working for it!

↘NOTES

Chapter Fifteen
Leadership

"Good leaders must communicate vision clearly, creatively, and continually. However, the vision doesn't come alive until the leader models it."

-John C. Maxwell

Throughout MLM, we believe we have a better way for the world. As a merchant of opinion, it would serve you to be an articulate speaker. This is also a quality that good leaders must possess. When you have confidence and command of language, you will definitely become a person of the people. The more you build these muscles of self-confidence, the stronger a leader you will be... sometimes. I leave this window open because I have known a very small percentage of good presenters who were terrible leaders, speaking with conviction about the company in front of the room while preaching doubt and fear in the hallways. This is <u>NOT</u> good leadership. You take the mic, you take the responsibility; that's the end of the story.

As a presenter, you are exposed to many different people. You have the chance to understand them, offer advice, give encouragement, and provide direction. Speakers should engage in presentations and talks with new people as often as they can. If you are choosing this path, this will help you strengthen your conversation skills and your leadership. As you are exposed to many different people, you will become sensitive to their ideas, questions, and wants. A presenter with great leadership traits can anticipate what the audience is curious about and take preemptive steps to address these in the presentation before they become questions unanswered in the parking lot!

For a person who wants to earn leadership respect through speaking, there are personal benefits you could gain while working to accomplish this:

- **The skill to listen is enhanced**
  - When you are the presenter, it does not mean that you only do the talking. In times when your audience gets the chance to ask you questions, you should be able to pull from the opinions or ideas of others.

- **Sensitivity and communication skills are developed**
  - Through this version of public speaking, you are able to explore communication lines you may have

never noticed before, or have never had the chance to really practice.

- **Unseen talents are discovered**
  - Presentations may lead you to the realization that you do have some things to explore about yourself and all the other factors that could affect your communication skills and growth as a social being.

- **You can fully grasp the power of your voice**
  - With this, you will be delving more into what it truly means to communicate. This is a great start for your own self-improvement!

These are only some of the benefits to improving your leadership when you **Present Like A Pro**.

⬂NOTES

Chapter Sixteen
Last Words

> *"I've missed more than 9,000 shots in my career. I've lost almost 300 games. 26 times, I've been trusted to take the game-winning shot and missed. I've failed over and over and over again in my life. And that is why I succeed."*
>
> -Michael Jordan

Eloquence is a great gift, and if you have it, you can affect lives and motivate people. The power of sharing with passion is very strong. Many great speakers have reshaped the world with their speeches. However, in our business, we do not have to be one of those great speakers on day one. You must be willing to be *bad* until you become *good*, until you are *great*, and just maybe one day you will be a *legend* in your company! As for now, start by scheduling your next meeting, being bold, and sharing your life-changing opportunity as your perfectly imperfect self.

Let's change the world with words...

Bonus Chapter:

On the Playground of Multilevel Marketing, the 'Teeter-Totter' Is Nothing to Play With!

[I n September of 2011, this article was published on ezinearticles.com. I received such positive feedback on it from everyone—from new sellers to seasoned industry veterans—that I wanted to include it for you, my readers and friends, in the hopes that it will improve your experience as a network marketer. It has been freshly edited and updated, although you can find the original at the web address listed at the end of this chapter. I hope you enjoy reading it as much as I enjoyed writing it!]

Something huge has just occurred to me about my life as a network marketer. Now, I'm a straight shooter, so please don't expect this to be pretty and refined. Understand that my goal is to help people who, like myself, want to seriously participate in network marketing while maintaining another job or business.

But let's get a definition out of the way first. For those who don't know, a teeter-totter (also known as a seesaw or teeter board) is a long, narrow board pivoted in the middle so that, as one end goes up, the other goes down. You'll normally see children playing on these at playgrounds or parks; they're just as much of a staple as slides or swing sets.

If you're reading this, I'm going to assume that you're involved in MLM or are seriously considering getting involved with a company. Most people in the part time arena of network marketing may never realize that they have placed their traditional career on one side and their MLM business on the other end of a giant teeter-totter.

How can this be? Let's say you were supporting yourself before you found the magic of this Industry, but if you share even a fraction of the excitement I first felt when I saw the earning potential and residual income it can create, you may have jumped into it cannon ball-style. I made a huge splash when I joined my company, and must say I was very happy about it. I was talked about, given recognition, and created a high growth organization at lightning speed. However, time and attention are finite things with limits, so when I started to dedicate most of my focus to my new business, have a guess at where my attention was dwindling.

The highly successful and generously lucrative private enterprise that I created from the ground up six years prior was being all but completely overlooked. The same thing that made me a successful candidate for my sponsor to recruit me into his business, I was ignoring as if it were an old shirt with a stain I couldn't wash out. Fast forward a year later and I realized that the income I was generating in my new business was not nearly enough to sustain my lifestyle, and that my traditional business was suffering tremendously due to a lack of leadership. Guess what I did. You got it—I hopped over to the other side of the teeter-totter and began rebuilding my company with both guns blazing.

Beyond the fire and smoke of my corporate comeback, my MLM organization began to become stagnant, and in some areas fall apart. The author of *The Compound Effect*, Darren Hardy, would have probably yelled, "Holy smokes! You lost big, Mo!" Who is Mo? Momentum is his full name; he is the invisible guy responsible for keeping a team and business motivated in an upward direction. Thus, the penalty for my lack of attention was a few fragmented groups of steadfast leaders amongst a sea of dead driftwood "tryers". There wasn't enough on either side of my teeter-totter to write home about.

So this repeated itself in what seemed to be an infinite loop for about two years. Although I did reach the National Director level at my company, I knew I needed an additional financial vehicle in my portfolio to protect the future of my family. I loved my company and the lifestyle it afforded me. Then, after many thousands of dollars and hours lost, I fixed it!

On a visit to see my friend Shane Tate, who was incarcerated at the time, he shared with me some very simple principles of life as he saw it. Under the stories of his situation, I learned the key to getting my situation under control. It was not taking a break from either one, because I had proven to myself on multiple occasions that abandonment ended in tragedy. It was organized, dedicated, unrelenting attention to BALANCE. Many people think they understand this and say, "After I get this other thing working again, I can focus on both." That kind of thinking is WRONG! The minute you leave the sanctity of that perfect sweet spot that keeps both ends of your business board up, as Lauren Hill would say, "You just lost one."

So let's wrap this thing up. You must continue to move forward in life while protecting what you already have. Don't go so hard at something new that you forget what got you where you already are. At the same time, if you become complacent in where you are, one day you may wish you had somewhere else to go. When one side of your teeter- totter begins to go down, resist the temptation to jump over to the other side. Simply scoot your butt closer to the middle until everything levels off.

| *"If I have helped one, then my job is done."*

-Lerrod Smalls

I think therefore I am.
I'm grateful therefore I have.
I love therefore I live Life on my own terms,
Helping others achieve success.
Failure Is Not An Option.

Article Source: http://EzineArticles.com/6597101

About the Author

Lerrod Smalls is an accomplished New York City entrepreneur, professional networker, and personal development trainer. With corporate experience as a former I.T. consultant to a Fortune 100 bank and serial entrepreneur, he has more than 15 years of real world business experience. As founder and CEO of a successful online supermarket and the enormously popular SANDBOX Pack and Ship retail store brand, Lerrod has been proven to invent and develop enterprises from his ideas.

Joining the industry of MLM in 2008, he has become a top producer with an Inc. 500 Network Marketing Company. His reputation for excellence and services is strengthened by the support he gives others, helping people grow within and outside of his direct organization. Top selling author and multimillion MLM earner King Pinyin said, "The thing I love about Lerrod is that he gives from his heart and truly wants everyone to succeed."

As a professional speaker, he has commanded the stage in front of thousands for motivating sales presentations and personal development trainings. Sharing on a variety of topics from corporate synergy training to commencement speeches, Lerrod is one of those rare individuals who can connect with anyone.

An advocate for the profession of network marketing, Lerrod regularly conducts interviews and submits articles educating on related subjects. From the position of entrepreneur, activist, husband, and father of two, he has gained recognition in national media as a prosperous business developer and success coach.

Prominent in his community, Lerrod is affectionately known throughout his hometown of Brooklyn by his last name, 'Smalls'. Lerrod has not only been recognized for his financial philanthropy, but also for his time as a Brooklyn Cub Scouts leader, NYC Summer Youth Program employer, Federal Bureau of Correction Half-way House program employer, and @Risk teen counselor. It is evident in his social works that Lerrod Smalls lives by the philosophy of 'service to many leads to greatness', yet he remains focused on profitable business endeavors and industries which are both socially conscious and provide regenerative value to the world.

About Dr. George Fraser

A s Chairman & CEO of FraserNet, Inc., Dr. George C. Fraser is the world's foremost authority on networking and building effective relationships. His career spans decades of accolades, and his childhood story of personal triumph is nothing short of inspiring.

A popular speaker and nationally recognized leader and innovator, he founded the *Power*Networking Conference —the nation's largest gathering of black professionals, business owners, and community leaders—and is the author of *Success Runs In Our Race, Race For Success*, and *Click*. He has been featured in such high profile print media outlets as *The New York Times, The Wall Street Journal,* and *USA Today.* Moreover, he has made over 250 radio and television appearances, including appearances on CNN Live, PBS, The Lou Dobbs Show, and Black Entertainment Television. Personal growth guru Stephen Covey calls George Fraser a "masterful teacher". And each year, tens of thousands of people attend his seminars and conferences to learn how to move beyond networking and start truly connecting to take their relationships to the next level.

I've been truly blessed to develop many valuable relationships with exceptional people in my life. I consider Dr. George Fraser as one to lead that list. Like so many others, I've followed his career and attended his speaking engagements, never failing to be moved by his incredible presentation power. Our connection became solid when I read his book Click and learned the secrets that have made him a worldwide authority on networking. I'm honored to have Dr. Fraser as a part of this book, and I hope this is a testament to young networkers and writers to seek out our great leaders as mentors.

-Lerrod Smalls

Excerpt from FraserNET.com

While George's accomplishments are significant, his beginnings were very humble. **He was born in Brooklyn, NY into a family of 11 children (8 boys and 3 girls).** When George's mom became mentally ill, his dad, a cab driver, could not care for 11 children, so **George was orphaned at 3 and spent 14 years in foster homes.** Growing up on the streets of New York, he had little hope and no expectations.

Although his guidance counselor suggested he drop out of high school, George graduated with a vocational diploma in woodworking because the school system did not consider him college material. Thank God George felt differently... For several years, he mopped floors on the midnight shift at LaGuardia Airport, while paying his way through college.

Later, in 1996, he graduated from the prestigious Dartmouth College Minority Business Executive Program. In 1999, **he was awarded the Honorary Doctorate Degree of Humane Letters from Jarvis Christian College.**

Dr. Fraser rose to leadership positions with Procter & Gamble, the United Way, and Ford Motor Company. It was some 25 years ago that God unveiled His real purpose for George. Mr. Fraser went on to author four critically acclaimed books: *Success Runs In Our Race: Complete Guide to Effective Networking in the African American Community*; *Race For Success: The Ten Best Business Opportunities for Blacks In America*; *Click: Ten Truths for Building Extraordinary Relationships*; and, most recently, a children's book titled **Who Would Have Thunk It: The First Adventures of The Fraser Foster Kids.**

Dr. Fraser is also the publisher of the award-winning **SuccessGuide Worldwide: The Networking Guide to Black Resources.** He is the founder of the national annual **PowerNetworking Conference**, where thousands of black professionals, business owners, and community leaders gather to learn the art and science of networking, entrepreneurship, and wealth creation.

Dr. Fraser is the Chairman of Phoenix Village Academy, which consists of three afro-centric charter schools serving Cleveland inner-city children. A popular speaker and author, George C. Fraser's inspiring talks on success principles, effective networking, wealth creation, business ethics, and valuing diversity are as popular among corporate professionals as they are among college students.

His views have been solicited by media as diverse as CNN and the *Wall Street Journal*. Over the past decade, the prestigious publication **Vital Speeches of the Day** has selected, reprinted, and distributed worldwide five of Dr. Fraser's speeches—a first for any professional speaker in America, regardless of color.

UPSCALE magazine named him one of the "Top 50 Power Brokers in Black America". *Black Enterprise Magazine* called him "Black America's

#1 Networker" and featured him on a cover issue. Dr. Fraser has appeared on seven national magazine covers and was recently inducted into the **Minority Business Hall of Fame and Museum**.

TV host and journalist Tavis Smiley called him a "visionary with the rare combination of leadership and management skills." Mr. Fraser was featured in the New York Times bestseller *Masters of Networking* along with Secretary Colin Powell.

Dr. Fraser has been married to Nora Jean for 40 years. They have two sons, Kyle and Scott.

To contact George C. Fraser, call (216) 691–6686 x201 or email him at gfraser@frasernet.com.

Credits

You are my business partners, my comrades, my confidants, and my friends. I recognize you as the many necessary characters, all acting as heroes in the movie of my life. Some roles may appear to be smaller than others, but you have all helped in a significant way. I would not be where I am, or who I am, without my 'Click'.

Adrien Boney
Ajamu Cummings
Ajay Gupta
Alvin Peters
Angela Sarro
Antonio Brooks
Arkell Cox
Aurelia Mack Family
Barry Donaldson
Bayo Simmonds
Bernadette Evans
Bert Girigorie
C.Anthony & Donna Harris
Cedric Lauchner
Charles A. Parker
Chassidy Elliott

Chorn Grandison
Chris & Paula DelosReyes
Cindy Bagwell
Claytisha Walden
Curt & Tishina Anderson
Darren Aronow
Darryl Huckaby
David Motivator Pharel
Davino Richardson
Dawnell Schofield
Dennis & Francine Nelson
Donna Phillips
Dorien Jones-Smalls
Douglas Minton
Dwayne & Carlene Eddings
Everton Welch

Eric Thomas
Glen & Kali Caldwell
Glen & Tonya Younge
Henry Nelson
Howard Toomer
Inelle Cooper
Jamaal & Kamilla Cooper
James Deloius
Jasper Brewster
Jeneen Barlow
Jerome & Leigh Crutch
John & Dawn Tadloc
John & Kathy Smalls
Jovens Moncouer
Judy Martin
Kamilla Collier
Keith White
Kenesha Traynham Cooper
Kenrick Scott
Kevin Brown
Khye & Ryan Goings
Kinja Dixon
Ladonya Brown
Lance & Karmit Cooper
Latrice Lyde
Lesley Derenoncourt
Libbie Booker
Lino Solis
Lisa Nicole Cloud
Mark & Kiet Bordley
Mark & Shedettah Richards

Marty & Isra Wynn
Meika Joseph
Melba Bermudez
Michelle Gall
Milton Davis
Mondez & Kayla Holloman
Nadina & Jean
Nicole Dotson Hewitt
Odelia McSween
Omarra Byrd
Oscar Solis
Paul Sealy
Penny & Sam McCullmn
Peter Huggins
Ricardo Suber
Richelle Williams
Robert Brown
Robert Cummins
Ron & Kathy Novotny
Sadiq & Crystal Coleman
Shaun Perkins
Shea & Shawn Flemming
Shireen Nelson
Stan & Chereace Richards
Steve & Nadia Delerme
Steve & Pasha Carter
Sunny & King Pinyin
Tammy Walking stick Riley
Tani Chambers
Ted Crawford
Tewan Lowe

Thomas Lytel
Tiffany Muff Cooper
Tillman & Lisa Doe
Todd & Kate Henches
Tupac Derenoncourt
Velda Flemming
Warren & Lennear Evans

Contact Information

WWW.LERRODSMALLS.COM

WWW.PRESENTLIKEAPRO.NET

FACEBOOK.COM/LERRODSMALLS

TWITTER.COM/LERROD

More information about George C. Fraser can be found at

WWW.FRASERNET.COM

www.ingramcontent.com/pod-product-compliance
Lightning Source LLC
Chambersburg PA
CBHW060036210326
41520CB00009B/1153